A Tribute to Remembrance

Jasmin Ring

BookLeaf
Publishing

Presentation by *BookLeaf Publishing*

Web: www.bookleafpub.com

E-mail: info@bookleafpub.com

ISBN: 978-93-95784-49-8

First edition 2022

DEDICATION

I dedicate these poems to all who strive to protect the freedoms of the world.

Let your sacrifices and stories echo through the halls of history for millennia to come.

Overwhelming Sacrifice

A solitary bird sweeps across the sky
The poppies sway in the gentle breeze
The crunch of boots fills the air
An endless column of young men
Weaves across the picturesque countryside

In an instant, the peaceful illusion is shattered
The sky fills with something sinister
Deadly bombs, falling without regard for the
lives below
The column collapses, survival trumps duty and
order
Loyalty evaporates, replaced by
self-preservation

Each bobbing helmet guards a loved one
Hopes, passions, fears - death cares not
Despair fills the air
Some who willingly came, prepared for the
ultimate sacrifice
Are now filled with regret

Time passes

The landscape is quiet again

Destruction and agony remain, death hangs in
the air
Country, creed, or religions bears no relevance
here
Stillness returns to the ravaged land
Men at war are now boys at rest

Vignettes of Battle

War
A constant among mankind
Avoidable yet engrained
Changing the fabric of society
Unravelling countless lives

The sounds
Silence as haunting cacophony
Explosions in the air above
Fear through unhuman sounds
A constant whirr of machines

The scents
Smoke, ash, embers
The burning of hopes and dreams
Despair and longing
Tarnished ground

The sights
Unimaginable horrors
Heroes among the destruction
Evil in human-form
Senseless sacrifice

An overwhelming sense
Of human hopelessness
Struggling to emerge
Victorious
But at what cost...

Empty Hearts

Distance makes the heart grow fonder...
Or so it has been said
Yet time and space evoke much more
. . . sleepless nights
. . . weariness
. . . yearning
. . . fear of "the knock"
. . . ever-widening disconnect

A soldier sacrifices much for their country
As do those left behind at home
Endless waiting, countless worries
The unknown looming endlessly
Craving the promised reunion

Too often, a desired left unfulfilled
A marble headstone in place of
A beloved warrior

Strangled by War's Clutches

The black charred remains / Faces cloaked in choking dust
of once thriving towns / Peer out of the rubble
Looming like specters in the dark
Devoid of all humanity

Schoolyards empty,children are gone / Those that persevere, are s
But hospitals are full / Alive, yet hardly living
Cemeteries crowded, yet silent
Churches empty - where has God been?

The landscape is scarred / Abandoned in desolation
Like the souls of its people / Choking on hopelessness
Broken, hurt, neglected
Showing the price of war

Watercolours of War

Crimson . . .
. . . poppies dancing in the field
. . . innocent blood spilled

Aquamarine . . .
. . . rolling, glistening waves
. . . wide open skies

Tan . . .
. . . uniforms proudly worn
. . . blowing desert dust

White . . .
. . . image of innocence
. . . flag of surrender

Green . . .
. . . rows of tanks
. . . forest refuges

Black . . .
. . . eyes witnessing horrors
. . . waves of despair

A mosaic of experiences

War Fever

He stands gazing skyward
Counting the miles, imagining the distance
Poised to enter the fight
Freedom for all
Only a month passes
The guided are now the guides
More deaths, more promotions
Soldiers evolve, not by choice
But out of necessity
A battle veteran
Propelled by the actions
Of those around him
Morals and dignity are lost
In the void
You are
Consumed by the fever
Instigated by war

A Soldier's Regret

Oh where, oh where is my guiding light?
Help me find my way out of this darkest night

There is no adventure, no newfound glory
Why did I leave home? Dear parents, I'm sorry

War is no longer conducted in an honourable
way
Machines rule supreme, with our lives we pay

Gone are the days of order and class
All that remains requires prayers at mass

There is no light in the heart of war
How I wish I knew all of this before

Eternal Gratitude

The gentle flow
Of time
Passing by infinitely
Each generation
Further removed
By the decades
From the unfathomable
Sacrifice

May our youth
Never have to face
The terrors
- loss, uncertainty
Of those before us
Yet memory eternal
The past must remain
Let such destruction
Not be in vain

Day of Remembrance

Bells toll
Wreaths laid
Hymns echoing
Across bowed heads

The Last Post sounds
Prayers murmured
Medals glisten
Attention
Heels clack
Salute

For today is November eleventh
Canada's annual day of remembrance
Out from the shadows
The veterans emerge

The once young soldiers
Now stooped and elderly
Come alive amidst the pomp
Glimpsing their glory days
One more time

Remembrance isn't a passing moment
It's a way of living
In honour of the past
Lest we forget

Memories Revisited

Stories - a richness unmatched
Eyewitness accounts
Offer a window into the past
Souls bared

Veterans, carrying a lifetime of
memories
experiences
wisdom
Are the keepers of history

The pendulum of time
Swinging into infinity
The fire of firsthand tales
Soon to be extinguished

The shadows of the past
Flitting through society
Possessing such richness
Yet often overlooked

Ask the questions
Embrace the stories
Cherish the sharing
Before it is too late

A Legacy Commemorated

How do we remember
The sacrifices once made
What can begin to honour
Those who were unimaginably brave

A simple plaque on a wall
Streets and buildings named in tribute
To those who fought and fell
Their names preserved

Monuments towering over the countryside
The sheen of noble white marble
The Sorrowful Mother, head bowed
A striking tribute and hallowed hall

A weathered stone cenotaph
Nestled along a bustling street
Identifies the local folk
Who gave their lives for thee

A Boy Among the Crosses

The air fills with the soft silence of freshly fallen
snow
A calm comes over the world, time stands still
As a young boy slowly moves among the rows
In this often-overlooked local cemetery

As if in a trance, he glides to the farthest corner
Pausing in front of a pair of matching stones
In one sweeping motion, he kneels before them
Sinking into the mounds of icy snow

The two crosses bear identical names
A father and son, both fallen in battle
The boy's family, dead before he was born
Dying, so he could live free

Liberty Warriors

The dreams of modern freedoms actualize
Filling the hearts of the oppressed with hope
Fierce determination empowers the hopeless
The voices of morality rise united

The gallant struggle for change persists
Released is an essence of infectious quality
Which envelopes the world: a Renaissance, a
revival
The souls of a nation against the leaders of
oppression

The clash of forces echoes around the globe
Painting images of horror unleashed
Tyrants aim to smother and conceal
But up rises yet another martyr

A phoenix ascends from the ashes
Brilliance emerging from the smoldering embers
As it lifts its majestic head to the horizons
The fire still burns within

The fight for regeneration endures

The Victory Parade

Where are we today?
The Victory Parade!

The crowds gather early
Buzzing with anticipation
A bright crimson poppy
Pinned with adoration

Where are we today?
The Victory Parade!

The little children run to the front
Eager to see the marching feet
Stepping in unison to the beat
Of the military band

Where are we today?
The Victory Parade!

Veterans, young and old
Proudly wearing their uniforms
Honouring the sacrifices
Preserving the past

Where are we today?
The Victory Parade!

Generations of Service

A tiny face peers in
The forbidden closet door
Close like the lips
Of her father
Whenever she asks
For tales of war

There hangs the uniform
Proudly pleated and pressed
Glistening medals
Adorn the breast

As soon as she can
The young girl joins cadets
Dreaming of the day
She has her own epaulettes

History repeats
Time after time
Future generations
Fall into line

Homecoming Woes

The demons creep behind the eyes
Fueling the inner flames
Of sadness, incomprehension
The shell shock setting in

Nobody understands the internal battle
Their eyes have not seen
All that they know of war
Is that which they've read

Some soldiers physically come home
But as mere shells of themselves
The vacant stares, unseeing yet full
Bearing the weight of horrors untold

"Lucky fella, he made it home" they would say
Never understanding that often
He wished he had not lived
To see another day

The Poppy

P . . . reserve our past, bind it for the future
O . . . ffer our thanks, fountains of gratitude
P . . . roudly represent remembrance
P . . . rotect bygone times, eternal memory
Y . . . esterday shaping tomorrow

The Existence of Remembrance

How do we remember?
The contributions of those before us
Who lived through things beyond our greatest
imagining
Who sacrificed more than we can even
comprehend
The men and women who placed their desires
aside
And acted for the greater good and collective
need
Some may call it a higher calling
Others pursue glory and adventure
Some serve unwillingly, yet strive to protect
Their comrades in arms

Why is there war?
Why do we fight?
Age old questions
That echo across space and time
Destined to remain unanswered.